The Island

Doug Johnson

ISBN: 0692177531
ISBN-13: 978-0692177532

DEDICATION

This book is dedicated to my sweetheart
Patty Pope Johnson
And our Lord and Savior
Jesus Christ

CONTENTS

ACKNOWLEDGMENTS

A special thanks goes out to all the family and friends who have encouraged me to push forward, to finish this story and to publish it. This experience has been a great tool toward my personal healing and an ongoing discovery of the plan God has for my life.

1 THE CRUISE

The sun was out, and the sky a brilliant blue. Not a single cloud in sight and the gentle breeze tossed the hair softly around on my head. The fragrance of the salty air was richly familiar, and the sound of the distant waves echoed in my ears. Standing on the mountaintop looking back down to the beach below, my mind raced. The earth had circled the sun several times since I first climbed this mountain. What was it that continually drew me to this place?

Although it was not a place I would consciously choose to visit of my own will, time and again would find me here on the beach; walking along or sometimes just sitting and staring out over the ocean. It was mainly on what I would deem special days;

anniversaries, birthdays, holidays and the like. Although just days on the calendar, it seems that these days found me here more often than others. The beach was crowded on holidays like Christmas and Thanksgiving but on days like today, not as much.

After spending time on the beach, making my way up the side of the mountain, I would turn to gaze back at the scene below me, reflecting, for a moment, on why I was here yet again. Today was one of those days.

This is the story of how this tiny island with its majestic mountain and foreboding attitude was forever woven into the fabric of my life. I would like to share it with you.

It all began as we prepared to board a large sea-going vessel for a cruise around the world. We had dreamed of this day for a long time; my wife, Joanna, more than me but what woman doesn't love a vacation? She had been anticipating this trip since she was a little girl. Everything was perfect. All the details of planning and preparation she had made was now coming to fruition.

Eyes wild with excitement myself, I, too, looked forward to time away with the woman I loved. What adventures awaited us? Where would our ports-of-call take us. The exact itinerary was a great mystery. Signing up with not much forethought we were unaware of what our destinations would be or even how long our journey would take. We were just thinking it would be fun and daring. Of course, our family members advised us with caution, but we knew this is what we wanted, and no one would deter us from our journey. In love with one another, we were ready set sail and to take on the world and see what it had to offer us and what we could experience together.

Making our way toward the ship, Joanna's face was bright and only enhanced by her contagious smile. She had a way of lighting up a room when she entered it. She was one of those women that could turn heads when she arrived somewhere. She didn't believe it about herself but others could see it instantly. She was truly a pretty woman but more than that, beautiful on the inside as well; always stopping whatever it was that she was in the middle of to help someone in need; giving preference to others above herself.

Most everyone she met became instant friends, but then again, she was an easy person to love. She was faithful to serve in church and was always giving; her time, our finances, her life. She loved to assist others and hospitality was her gift. Her gifts were used wisely, and her greatest desire was to see those she loved experience God's love for themselves in a powerful way.

She spent time reading her Bible daily as was evidenced by the tattered edges of the pages. I remember trying to talk her into getting a new Bible once. She would have nothing to do with that notion. This Bible had become a friend and companion to her. She knew right where to turn for any situation and little notes in the margin made the book come alive with history and sermons she had heard over the years. She loved her Bible and no one was going to take it from her.

She was also a prayer warrior. She would always pray for friends who were going through tough times or who needed encouragement or who were sick. This was her prayer daily; that those she met and enjoyed life with would have the same type relationship she had with her Heavenly Father; one of continuing growth and maturity. Our morning prayer time always included prayers for our family members; especially our children and grandchildren.

We have three adult children and two grandchildren who all live close to our home, so, we could visit with them on a moment's notice; Often stopping by their house or they ours just to say hello or to have a cup of coffee.

Although Joanna loved everyone, these five people along with myself were her very heart. Family was so ultimately important to her; a trait passed down from her own parents I believe. She loved just spending time with family.

Pausing as we walked up the long gang plank to board the ship, I was able to take in Joanna's beauty and gather my emotions. The sun dress with brightly painted large flowers she had purchased for the trip was the perfect complement to her olive skin complexion. She was indeed radiant and the sparkle in her big brown eyes projected pure joy.

My mind wandered back to our wedding day watching as she in her beautiful wedding gown with her hand in her Daddy's arm walked down the aisle toward me. The dress was exquisite with lace bodice and tulle overlay. The intricate details of the lace were so graceful and delicate but were no match for Joanna's beauty. There was no one else in the world at that moment. That was over 30 years ago, and I still marvel at her beauty. I truly believe she got more beautiful as the years passed.

Joanna turned around quickly, *"Wayne, hurry up! We have lots to see and do!"* she said, snapping me back to reality. Smiling, so wide my cheeks hurt, I walked briskly to catch up with her, thankful that we didn't have to worry about the luggage. That surely would have made things a lot slower. Packing lightly was not in Joanna's skillset anyway, but a trip around the world combined with the fact that we didn't know how long we would be gone made a perfect recipe for over-packing. Let's just say we had a lot of suitcases to account for.

She took my hand in hers and we continued up the walkway to the ship. The way her hand fit perfectly in mine was almost as if our hands were made for one another. Often, she would tell me that she loved my hands; something about strength and protection. I didn't understand completely but knew it was a good thing. She would just sit and stroke my hands while we watched a movie or drove along in the car on one of our many outings we called adventures.

Thinking back now, they really weren't much of an adventure. These outings would entail flea markets, antique stores, farmer's roadside stands and the like. Mostly though, we would just grab a frozen coffee drink from the local coffee shop and take a drive out into the countryside and try to get lost before turning on our GPS to find our way back home. I would drive and every time we approached an intersection I would ask,

"*Which way?*" Joanna would typically respond with the "*turn right*" or "*turn left*" answer but if the roads were so rural that the county officials hadn't even bothered to paint lines on them, I knew that was the way she would want to go. She really loved the roads with no lines. "*That means we are really deep in the country,*" she would say.

Many times, as we drove along, she would see a field with a group of trees on a hill and say, "*I want a house right up there under those trees one day.*" We dreamt of owning a small plot of land one day, maybe five to ten acres, with a tree-lined drive, a white-railed fence and a ranch-style home on a slight hill overlooking a small lake or pond with the grandchildren playing all around. The home, of course, would have a large porch across the width of it, so we would have a place to put our rocking chairs. This would be a spot that we would drink coffee every morning, watch sunsets every evening, enjoy long conversations and just grow old together. But there would be time for all that after our cruise.

The ship was massive; towering above us. White and glistening in the sunlight, it was hard to imagine something that large could even float. Standing on the ground with the ship soaring stories over us brought a passing sentiment of smallness and insignificance to my mind. It's amazing how something so large and overwhelming can make you feel so small in comparison. I could imagine that's just a tiny fraction of what it will be like to stand before the very throne of God one day; overwhelmed by his greatness and our smallness.

On board the ship we wandered aimlessly while attempting to appear that we knew where we were going and what we were doing. It seems men are good at this trait, but, giving in to frustration after a bit, I finally asked for directions. Being the man that I am, I briefly hesitated to ask for help but Joanna had a way of making me feel comfortable with shortcomings and I had come to the place where things of this nature didn't bother me the way they did before I met her. *"We're not lost,"* Joanna would always say, *"we are just exploring a place we've never been."* The proverbial glass was always half-full to her.

A steward led us to the space where we would end up spending very little time. The room was well decorated but simple and smelled of imitation coconut. Our hosts had even put chocolate candies on our pillows and folded up the wash cloths and towels to resemble a small zoo. The cabin was an interior stateroom with no windows, but Joanna didn't mind. *"As long as we are together,"* she said, *"I'm happy. Plus, we've got too much to see and do outside this room to be worried about where we will sleep."* She continued talking about other things, but, her beauty overtook me once again and my ears didn't comprehend what she had said. *"You're my favorite,"* I interrupted. It was our special phrase; one of those little things that couples say to each other that become part of their lives and vocabulary. Joanna just smiled. Saying it made me feel warm and fuzzy inside and I relished how it made her smile. It was exactly how I felt though. And I know she appreciated it too. She had one dimple on her left cheek. I knew that when that dimple showed up, she was smiling sincerely. She was my favorite person in the world and my very best friend.

"You're not even listening to what I'm saying, are you?" She questioned. *"Who me?"* I asked with a smirk. *"Why don't we get our bags unpacked and take in the sights of the ship?"* I asked rhetorically. So that's what we did. Our luggage was emptied with clothes put away in the tiny compartments and we were out and about in no time at all. Although the ship had lots of things for entertaining its passengers, my favorite entertainment was to walk to the bow of the ship and just stare at the horizon with the wind in my face and the smell of the ocean in my nostrils. There was just something regal about the experience. The thought did

cross my mind to do the whole "Titanic" movie thing on the bow of the ship but I thought better of the idea and settled on just soaking in the salty air.

2 SICKNESS

The next few days and weeks on the ship became a blur of activity. We began to make a lot of new acquaintances along the way, some of whom would become lifelong "family-member" friends. You know, the folks that your children call uncle and aunt even though you are not blood-related. It's strange how you can meet someone and know almost instantly that this friendship was something special. That's the way we felt about a lot of the people who had crossed our path on this journey. Each one, on an adventure of their own, not knowing where they will end up at the other end of this trip but enjoying every day as if it were the last day of their journey. But, at the same time looking forward to new exploits ahead of them. Looking back now, I see how each of these individuals had been intertwined into our lives and the treasure that each one brought. It is amazing, and this trip would not have been the same without them.

Our days were spent browsing boutique shops on the ship or catching a movie in the oversized theater. Sometimes we would slip into the theater just to enjoy a large tub of buttered popcorn and disappear as quickly as the snack did and before the movie was over.

Oh, I almost forgot. The ship even hosted an art auction. Joanna thought that would be a fun event, so we attended, signed in, and received a bidder number. The number, 716, was printed in a large font on what appeared to be a ping-pong paddle. Not being art enthusiasts, I thought our wallet would be safe from the art thieves. Before I could get the bidder paddle away from Joanna, we owned several paintings. The day was enjoyable, however, and now we have these paintings in our home to enjoy and remember our trip. Every time we spoke of that day, it would always end in laughter.

Relaxing on the upper deck soaking in the sunshine with a good book is how many days were spent. Still others would be spent frolicking in the shallow calm waters at some exotic port of call. One day that was particularly memorable was the day we went snorkeling and then drove a dune buggy across a private island to a remote beach where a gourmet lunch was catered. We felt like royalty that day for sure.

There were great days such as these, some mundane, uneventful days and some not so good; for example, the time we both got so sunburned that we had to lay perfectly still in our cabin waiting for the pain to subside. Each of us taking turns coating the other with aloe gel. Or the time Joanna got stung by jellyfish while playing in the water. *"Ouch, ouch, ouch!"* I remember her yelling in rapid succession like she had just touched a hot stove. Jellyfish stings were the worst. How could something so graceful pack such a powerful punch? What did we ever do to them to deserve such attacks? Several home remedies, such as rubbing sand on the sting or coating the area with lemon juice, were used to no avail. No relief was found, and I remember thinking at the time that these remedies were just to keep us occupied until the stings subsided on their own.

There was also the time the captain of the ship came to us and let us know that another couple had decided to leave the ship and wanted to know if we would enjoy an upgrade to a room with a view. Of course, we accepted and rushed to gather our belongings and moved into an extremely nice room that was also well appointed. More than that was the incredible views of the ocean at sunrise and sunset.

The room opened onto a small but ample balcony deck. There were two teak wood lounge chairs and a small table with fresh flowers. We were able to enjoy more time in our suite now than before because of the views it offered. We spent many mornings on the balcony enjoying a cup of coffee and watched the stars pass by in the evenings. I had to wonder if this upgrade was somehow God's doing. It wouldn't surprise me if it was. He has a way of blessing us with things we want but haven't actually asked for. There were certainly more good times than bad. Our journey was definitely enjoyable. Life was good.

After enjoying a hearty meal with friends one evening on the promenade deck, it was the wee hours of the morning before conversation and laughter waned. Joanna and I made our way back to our new room feeling full and satisfied. We had genuinely had a splendid evening. Smiling at one another, each knew the other was feeling gratified with our journey. Making our way back to our suite, Joanna snuggled up next to me as we walked hand in hand. No words were necessary. We both knew what the other was thinking. "We are so in love with one another and life is so good. I don't want this feeling to ever end" I thought to myself. Cuddled up in the warm bed it was only a matter of minutes before exhaustion overtook us and we both fell fast asleep.

Unusual sounds coming from the bathroom a short hour later shook me from my slumber. Joanna was not feeling well and was hugging the toilet and vomiting violently. I rushed in to assess the situation. Her face was pale and tiny beads of sweat formed on her brow. I took a washcloth and soaked it with water and squeezed the excess away. Patting her face and neck with the cool cloth, my mind traveled back to a time just after we were married. In a similar situation and not sure what to do with a sick wife, I had asked Joanna what I could do for her. Her reply, "I just want my Mom." Although my countenance dropped, it did make me a better nurse the next time. We all still laugh when we recall that incident.

Smiling at the memory and hoping she wouldn't see I asked, "Is there anything else I can do for you?" "No," she said, "It was probably something I ate. I do feel better now that I got it out of my system. Let's just get back to bed; hopefully I'll feel better by morning." As we lay in the bed, Joanna's cold feet, like a magnet, were soon attached to the back of my thighs. I smiled quietly and drifted back to sleep.

3 SHOPPING

The next morning, somewhere between awake and sleep, I couldn't remember where I was for a moment. Suddenly, recalling the events of the prior evening, I reached over to touch Joanna only to realize she wasn't in the bed with me. I bolted upright in the bed as I gathered my thoughts. I called out to her. No answer. My eyes darted to the balcony thinking maybe she was having coffee, but she wasn't there either. It is not common for me to panic but a million questions flooded my mind. Where could she be? Did she get sick again and go to the ship's doctor? Did she sleep walk and leave the room? Did someone come in and take her while we slept? This was unusual for her to leave without letting me know. I jumped up and slipped into my shorts and t-shirt. As I exited the cabin, Joanna was coming toward me down the narrow hallway. *"Where have you..."* I began in a whisper-shout. Quickly putting her index finger over my lips, she whispered, *"Shhhhh! You're going to wake the other passengers."* Slipping back into our room as I asked, *"Where were you?" "I had to go get some air,"* she said. *"I was worried about you. How are you feeling this morning?"* I returned. *"I'm okay,"* she said, *"Just feeling a little nauseous still." "Can I get you something?"* I asked. *"Food? Water? Medicine?"* She just smiled and replied, *"Thank you honey, I'm going to be okay."* She told me she had gotten up earlier but didn't want to disturb me. She was able to find a few peanut butter crackers at the snack bar to settle her stomach. *"I'm really feeling much better."* With eyebrows raised, I gave that "husband-look" questioning the veracity of the statement. She recognized the look immediately. *"Honestly,"* she said, *"I do feel better."*

We had a way of communicating with one another that sometimes required no words. I guess a lot of married people are that way. It certainly makes conversation easy when you get to this point in a relationship especially for the men. Men do well with fewer words and just hand gestures or special looks.

The next two days were very busy; so busy that I had almost forgotten that Joanna had been feeling bad. Although she wasn't eating as well as normal, that could be the case with anyone who has had some stomach bug, so I discounted it to that. Our lives got back into routine and we moved forward with enjoying our journey.

Joanna asked if it would be okay if we went swimsuit shopping. The swimsuit she had brought along with us for the trip was older and showing signs of wear and tear and the elastic was beginning to give up. *"We wouldn't want Mr. Elastic to quit his job without notice."* I mused. *"Of course, we can go,"* I began with a smile, *"as long as we can get a little something for me too!"* Joanna just smiled back. She knew I enjoyed browsing and shopping as much as she did, and I usually could find something that "I just had to have." *"Remind me to look for a cover-up while we are out,"* Joanna added. Swimsuit cover-ups served one purpose; to cover women's nakedness while they jiggled from one point to another without everyone seeing every dimple, scar or extra pound. They surely didn't take away the flaws, just hid them from public exposure. I've found that men do the same thing, but, just use an old t-shirt to accomplish the same mission. *"I need to look for a t-shirt too,"* I replied smiling.

We browsed the little shops on the ship for a while and not being able to find what she was looking for, decided to go ashore to the small village where we were docked. The flip-flops I had brought along for the trip were worn to the point of rubbing blisters between my toes. As we were shopping, they finally gave up the fight and I found myself walking around without any shoes on my feet. Joanna came across a new pair for me and the price was right, so I slipped them on and tried to break them in.

Continuing our search for swimsuits and cover-ups, I noticed Joanna grimace and put her hand to her stomach. It had been over four days since she started feeling bad that first night. Surely this isn't the same bug she had before. *"What's wrong?"* I asked. *"Oh, it's nothing"* she replied, *"probably just some gas pains or bloating."* She passed it off as nothing, but I was becoming more and more concerned for her health.

As the ship's horn sounded in the distance announcing its soon departure, we hurried back with our only purchase being the new flip-flops. Finding a suitable swimsuit or cover-up had been a lost cause. It seemed that most of the swimsuit manufacturers are on some sort of fabric ration as the suits we did find were extremely skimpy. We decided to pick up our search at the next port.

4 THE STORM

Back on the ship it was late afternoon as we set sail headed straight into the setting sun. It was indeed beautiful. The way the sun bounced off the clouds in the distance made for a postcard-worthy photo opportunity. We stood on the bow of the ship that afternoon taking photos of one another and a few "selfies" with God's masterpiece as the backdrop.

The beauty was fleeting. Just a few short hours later, we found ourselves in somewhat of a gale. The seas became angry and the winds were howling. Although the massive ship is designed to weather this type of storm, it was all a bit unsettling to say the least. Hunkered down in our cabin, the ship tossed and rolled making even the strongest stomachs queasy. The sound of the rain pelting the sliding glass door on our balcony sounded like a Morse Code transmission with its dots and dashes.

We tried getting into bed early, but the motion of the ship made falling asleep futile. After a while the rain stopped pinging the glass of our balcony door but the wind continued to howl. Joanna was feeling sick to her stomach again. The decision was made to go out on the balcony to get some fresh air; assuming it was seasickness since I was not feeling all that well either. Once on the deck outside, we realized the winds were still blowing rather strong, but the rain had stopped. Everything around us was soaked and the deck was a little bit slippery. Looking down at the seas in the darkness of the night, the white-capped waves were highlighted by the lights of the ship and still in a tempest and looked intensely irritated.

Standing on our little balcony and holding tight to the railing, I must admit that I felt better just being out in the open with fresh air in my face. Joanna agreed. She, still though, was fighting the nausea that had seemed to come back with a vengeance. Without any warning, Joanna shrieked and doubled over in pain. At that exact instant, a giant wave caused the ship to dip and roll so that I lost my stomach; that same feeling in your stomach as you top that first hill on a roller coaster. In one smooth motion Joanna's feet slid out from under her and she lost her grip on the handrail. Before I knew what was happening, she went tumbling over the edge of the ship's railing toward the raging waters below.

Time froze momentarily. I did not know what to do. Staring over the edge of the railing I saw a great splash as she hit the water stories below. *"I should throw something overboard for her to hold on to,"* I thought. Instinctively, I grabbed the first thing that I could find, one of the lounge chairs sitting nearby, and tossed it overboard. Without further thought, I was up and over the railing and making the plunge down to the waters below myself.

Falling for what seemed an eternity, flashes of light from each level I passed thumped my eyes like strobe lights on a disco dance floor. Flailing my arms around and trying to keep my body vertical was to no avail. My ten-story belly-flop smacked the water with such force that it temporarily rendered me oblivious to my surroundings and took every ounce of air from my lungs. The furious water along with the ship's undertow drug me under and tossed and rolled me like a ragdoll in a cement mixer until I thought I would certainly perish. Surely, I was going to die, and I wondered how Joanna could have survived that fall as well. Breaking above the water my mouth gasped for air and was met by an angry wave crashing into my face causing me to take a deep breath of salt water into my lungs. Coughing and sputtering I was taken under the water yet again. Resurfacing a short time later, I yelled at the top of my lungs, *"Jo! Hang on baby! I'm coming to save you!"* Another wave. Another roll under the currents. Over and over the waves, as if I had stolen their lunch money, mustered a relentless attack on me. *"Joanna, where are you?"* I yelled again.

Suddenly, and without warning, a sharp blow to the back of my head caused me to see stars. As I felt the sting of the salty water and warm blood flowing from the back of my head down my neck, the whole world seemed to close in on me as if I was entering a tunnel. I turned around to see that the chair that I had tossed overboard earlier had come back to attack me as if it were angry at me for tossing it over. I latched on to the chair with all my might until my knuckles were completely white. Luckily the chair was floating and as soon as I located Joanna, she could have something to hold on to as well. *"Joanna!"* I yelled again. *"Jo!"*

Drifting in and out of awareness, I watched as the ship's lights grew smaller and smaller in the distance. The ship continued its course not knowing that it had lost two passengers. How long until they realized we were gone? How long will we be adrift out here? My thoughts turned back to Joanna. I frantically searched the horizon. Maybe she was floating nearby. Maybe she would pop to the surface soon. Although free from the undertow of the ship, the waves continued to abuse me; overturning the deck chair multiple times. Getting weaker from the loss of blood I yelled her name over and over until I eventually lost consciousness.

5 STRANDED

I must have been unconscious for a while. As I felt the sun on my face the next morning, I awoke to find myself in the breakers of a small lagoon with a sandy beach in front of me. This beach was different than any other I had ever seen. The waves were large and flung me up on the beach with such force that I felt as though I had been shot out of a canon. Loosening my grip on the chair that had both attacked me and saved my life, I drug it up onto the beach. The sand was a mottled dark gray color; almost black. Instead of just sand, it appeared that it was combined with broken glass and shards of pottery of unknown origins. With the rough shards and sharp gravel gouging my hands and knees, I crawled up on the beach and gingerly rolled over to my back side. I sat for a few moments staring back out across the vast ocean in front of me. Large waves rising out of the ocean and crashing just a short distance offshore told me that there was probably a coral reef of some kind out there. The waters in the lagoon were certainly a bit calmer but the whitecapped waves collided violently with the shore dumping more of those glass shards with each thunderous crash. My head was throbbing from the wound caused by the chair and my hair was matted with blood. I remember thinking it was a miracle that I had not been eaten by a shark during the night.

A thought suddenly invaded my mind, *"Maybe Joanna made it to safety on the beach as well."* Jumping up, I began running along the shore looking for any signs of footprints or life. I noticed for the first time, my flip flops were lost in the battle at sea. Sadness about the flip-flops temporarily rushed in but my thoughts turned back to Joanna. Running along the beach, the glass shards wreaked havoc on my feet as if running through a minefield of broken glass. Each plant of a foot caused my own weight to create vicious slices comparable to a musketeer gone wild with his Claymore. What would normally take an hour took several as I made my way gingerly around the island hobbling like a young boy running barefoot across hot asphalt in July. I was calling out her name over and over. By the time I had returned to the lounge chair, my feet and toes were bleeding profusely, and I was in a great deal of pain. What were these glass remains on the shore? Where did they come from?

Nursing my feet the best I could and surveying my surroundings, I realized that the beach where I washed up was a small island in a crescent shape; what appeared to be an outcropping of a long-ago active volcano probably rising out of the ocean back when dinosaurs roamed the earth. I suppose if the reef off shore were visible above the water, the island would look like a doughnut. The high, jagged black cliffs behind me, glistening and slick, disappeared into steely gray clouds above. No signs of life. No signs of Joanna anywhere. Just the relentless sound of the ocean waves breaking over the reefs and making their way to the beach.

Turning my thoughts to survival, I began an assessment of my situation. Certainly, water and shelter would need to take priority. As a hummingbird whizzes quickly from flower to flower, my mind bolted back and forth from question to question. What about food? How long would I be here? How will I survive? Where is Joanna? Searching the beach and into the edge of the vegetation I gathered items that would make a good shelter. The sun was hidden from view by the overbearing dark clouds above, but the sun would be out soon, and I would need protection from it. Pausing again to look across the beach to the lagoon, the waves just off shore continued their assault on the reef and the sound was constant and deafening. The way the sun was obscured by the dark clouds above gave an ominous chill to the island as a tapestry being stirred by the wind in some abandoned haunted house. I could see that the sun was shining out on the ocean, but, my island was dark and gray and likened to one of those old black and white horror movies I remembered from my childhood.

Gathering enough driftwood to construct a crude shelter frame, I used palm branches for protection from the sun. Additional palms would make for a bed once evening came. Surely the sun would not be obscured by these clouds for long. The search for water found nothing but salty pools around the breakers. Scaling the side of the mountain was inevitable to find some sort of water source. Navigating the steep cliff edges was tremendously challenging. The rocks were razor sharp, slick and unusually jagged. Climbing just a little way left my hands cut and bleeding in several places. Scaling the cliff face was likened to trying to climb the edge of a serrated knife blade. I was, however, able to find a small pool in the rock crevices where rainwater had collected and, even though the water was warm, it was so refreshing to take a drink of fresh water. I had not realized how parched I was until the water touched my tongue.

Thoughts drifted to the convenience of water. Access was simple. Just walk to the refrigerator and crack open the lid to a plastic bottle. Remembering back on how I had gotten angry once because Joanna had forgotten to get the bottled water at the grocery made me feel guilty. Having to drink water straight from the tap was unacceptable. Just thinking how selfish I had been made my heart sink. How I ached for a drink of cool water; even water from the garden hose right now would be okay.

How I missed Joanna too. I remembered fondly the time we had a water fight while washing her car one Saturday afternoon. We splashed and hosed one another until I tackled her gently and we rolled in the grass laughing until our sides hurt.

I had to devise a plan to take some of this water back down to the shelter for when she showed up. I knew she would be thirsty too. *"The lounge chair has a vinyl-covered pillow,"* I remembered aloud. Surely that would hold water. I retreated to my crude shelter with plans to take the pillow cover up the following day and fill it with water.

The next few hours were spent trying to start a fire. I had watched on several television survival shows how survivalists would just rub some sticks together and in a matter of minutes, have a roaring fire. That was not my case. With hands already bleeding, I attempted several methods to get at least a puff of smoke to appear. Darkness was overtaking the island before I was able to get a spark and get a fire going. Soaked in sweat and hands sore and bleeding, I felt a sense of accomplishment that I assume can only come from overcoming such conflict.

That night, as I lay on my bed of palm fronds staring at the night sky, I longed for that small cabin with no windows with Joanna nestled up next to me. I looked at my hands by the light of the small fire and thought about what Joanna had said about strength and protection. As I turned my hands to look at the backs of them, I thought to myself, *"Some protector I have been."*

Looking up into the darkness, I gathered that the dark cloud that had covered the island during the day had been relieved of its duty by an inky blackness of the night sky. Gazing toward the sky and wondering where the stars were hiding, complete and utter loneliness overtook me; as if someone had unplugged my heart and turned out the lights in my life. I wondered if God was around tonight. I certainly did not "feel" his presence. Longing for someone, anyone, to talk to but nothing. No one was there. No one was listening. Certainly, my ending up on this island was not God's doing. After all, he is a loving God, right?

6 DISCOVERY

Perched under my temporary shelter the next day, I saw something floating in the shallow waters where the waves were breaking on the shore. Slipping tentatively down to the water's edge, I noticed not one, but two flip-flops and once I retrieved them, realized they were the exact ones I had lost the night before. At least I would be able to walk the beach to look for supplies.

Sliding the shoes onto my feet I made a trek along the beach looking for anything that could help with my survival. Even with the minimal protection of the shoes, the sharp remnants on the beach continued to nip at the sides of my feet and heels. Tiny cuts, like paper cuts, appeared around each foot and the sting of the salt water quickly defeated my resolve of discovering any useful items along the beach. Walking a bit further but finding nothing of benefit to my survival, I retreated to my little makeshift hut on the beach.

Another full day had passed finding me sitting in the shelter feeling sorry for myself. Many questions, like missiles, continued their fusillade on my mind. Where is Joanna? Is she still alive? Will she be walking up the beach any moment now? Maybe the ship found her, and she is now searching frantically for me. Crying again, the questions continued. Why was I weeping? Why am I feeling this way? I didn't want to admit it but the thought of possibly losing Joanna was becoming more real with each passing moment. Surviving the fall and the ocean turbulence seemed far-fetched for someone of her stature.

Time seemed to be passing so slowly; much too slowly for me; walking, praying and promising. Making promises to God was rather dumb and irrational I know, but I couldn't help it. Finding Joanna safe was all I could focus on and my mind was being consumed by it. Shaking these feelings off, I began to focus on getting off this island alive. Finding myself walking along the beach searching for driftwood or other items of significance, my focus had finally shifted to survival mode. I had decided to brave the cuts on my feet and get out there to see what had washed ashore that would be beneficial to my survival. What I would find on this specific day, however, I was ultimately unprepared for.

Walking along the shore with my feet in ankle deep water, the focus was on looking for food more than driftwood. My stomach was aching from lack of nourishment and surely I could find some seafood to eat. I observed small clam-like mussels burrowing in the sand with each retreating wave.

Reminded of an article I had read recently, I remembered that these exact clams were a delicacy on some island nations. The local islanders would gather the clams and lay them in the sun until the mussels opened up. At this point, the clams were popped into their mouths without so much as a courtesy rinse in water. They would certainly be a boost of protein for me. Not being a fan of sushi, I would have to at least show the clams to the fire first. I've always felt they should call sushi what it is; bait.

While focusing on digging the clams, movement down the beach caught my eye. I stood up, put my hand over my brow and peered down the beach. Squinting, I remembered I had never gone for that eye doctor appointment Joanna had been on my case about. I needed glasses to clearly see things that were distant, but, I kept delaying the appointment. It would help if I had some glasses now I thought. Joanna was right; I should have heeded her instruction. Again.

Even with the gloomy, overcast skies and my vision lacking, I could see something floating at the edge of the water. My heart sank to the bottom of my stomach. What was it? Could it be? The few clams I had gathered hit the ground with a thud as I broke into a sprint down the beach toward it. Closing the gap, the realization hit me that it was, undeniably, a person floating in the surf with a sun dress similar to the one owned by my precious Joanna. Rushing into the thigh-deep water I crumpled to my knees fearing what I would see and at the same time knowing that the beautiful sun dress was definitely hers. Turning her over confirmed my darkest fear; it was my precious Jo. She was lifeless. Dead. Gone.

Even though she had been in the water for a couple of days now, and her face showing signs of decay, she looked peaceful somehow and still beautiful. I dragged her into my arms and began to moan and cry uncontrollably. Finally, able to muster an intelligible word, *"Nooooo!"* I screamed in half words and half sobs. *"This is not real. This can't be real,"* I kept telling myself. Not wanting it to be true, still, the finality of the situation was penetrating my soul. Kneeling in the breakers, the sea taunted me with continuous prods and pokes with each incoming wave just like a bully on an elementary school playground. My hatred for this placed boiled.

Memories are sporadic, but, I do remember gathering Joanna up in my arms and carrying her lifeless body up onto the beach away from the pounding surf careful not to let her body get damaged further from the jagged pieces of glass and pottery on the beach. Even though she was dead, my protector instinct was in full force. Maybe I was just trying to make up for what I was unable to do the night she fell overboard. Time stood still. I felt as if someone had plunged a needle full of Novocain into my heart and drugged me because the next few hours are just a vague memory of numbness with a foggy-headed recollection of what exactly took place.

Once I came to my senses, my eyes burned from the crying and my nose ran like an old drippy faucet. I carried Joanna up to the edge of the canopy near a solitary palm tree. This is the place where I would bury my wife.

I spent the next couple of hours digging a pit with my hands. Great drops of sweat mixed with tears fell into the makeshift grave as I dug. Stopping frequently to shoo the flies away from Joanna's body, I wondered where all these flies came from. There had not been any insects around since I landed here a few days ago.

Once I got the hole in the ground to about four feet deep, I could not physically go any further and thought this was probably deep enough. Who decided that six feet was the standard grave depth anyway? Gathering Joanna's body up in my arms, I carried her over and gently placed her in the grave. I sat, exhausted, in the bottom of the pit next to her and held her hand.

I slipped her wedding band off her finger and shoved it down in my pocket. It was right then that I wished someone would just take a bulldozer and push all that sand right on top of both of us. Death was welcome, and I would have gone willingly. The next few minutes were spent trying to make her look her best. I stroked her hair and brushed the sand away from her face and arms shooing flies all the while.

Staring at her there, it appeared as if she were sleeping peacefully and would awaken at any moment. I waited for a few moments before climbing out of the grave and looking back down once again, I couldn't make myself push the sand over her lifeless body and cover her up. In my mind it was as if covering her up was admitting reality; that the finality of the whole situation could be avoided if I didn't. I turned away and fought back tears again. Wrestling with these thoughts, my logical side kicked in and I realized that I had to cover her. With the decay and now fighting flies, it was the best thing. Sitting down beside the pit I placed my feet facing one side. With all my strength I dug my heels in and pushed an immense amount of sand over into the pit. With my eyes closed I continued to kick and push with my feet until the ground was level again. I smoothed out the surface the best I could and made it look presentable. I buried my wife on that island. Thirty-five years of wedded bliss and this was how it was to end. Tears flowed again.

To conduct a small funeral, my emotions had to be reined in. The eulogy was simple; thanking Joanna for the time she gave me and told her once again that she was, and always would be, "my favorite." I cried some more. A rough stone was used to mark her grave. Walking out to the beach, I picked up one of the glass shards and came back up to scratch her name on the stone. The shard made a great tool in my hand to put all the relative information on the crude headstone. I remembered back to a sermon I had heard once about the dash between the birth and death dates and how we must make the most of the "dash" in our lives. Our whole life story is wrapped up in that dash; every experience, memory, laughter, tear and adventure. It is also a reminder of how short our lives are here on this earth. Just a vapor and then you pass away.

After I had finished, and admiring my work, I looked down and noticed my hand was bleeding. The sharp edges of the shard had cut my hands while using it to inscribe the stone. My plans were to dig her body up once I was rescued and give her a proper burial back home. Life would never be normal again, not that any life is ever normal. But, it would be so different and empty without her.

7 THE GREAT ANGER

Joanna's grave now behind me and standing near my shelter, I stared out over the horizon for what seemed an eternity. Suddenly, and without warning, my heart exploded. A flash flood of emotion, releasing pent-up anger down the dry, stony canyon of my soul.

Turning my eyes heavenward, a sound unfamiliar to human ears started from my toes, coursed through my body and exploded off my tongue. It was a guttural-type growl, but, with a violence that I had never experienced that came from my mouth. *"Why? Why did you let this happen? Why did you take Joanna from me? Why did you let me wash up here? Wasn't it enough that you killed my wife? Now you want to torture me on this island too?"* Anger was at its boiling point. Picking up the nearest thing I could find, a large piece of driftwood, a makeshift club, I began swinging it with all my might destroying everything within reach. My small shelter took most of the punishment. Groans and moans of despair along with fury spat through my lips as I beat everything in sight. In a frenzy, I pounded out my rage until I was exhausted and spent. Slumping to the ground in a pile that resembled a pile of dirty laundry, I cried and screamed until I was unable to lift my head any longer. Even in my exhaustion, my anger seethed, and I continued my verbal assault through tears, until my voice was hoarse and raspy.

Overwhelming agony had overtaken me while I lay on the beach that night and the sense of loss was unexplainable. I was breathing, but not alive, not even certain how long I was there with my head in my hands.

I'm sure that everyone who's lost someone dear goes through similar feelings and emotions but no two can be exactly alike. Each relationship and person are different so each one grieves differently. Thinking back to times when friends of mine lost a loved one I recollected how I had said, *"I know how you feel,"* or *"Man, that must be rough."* What a lack of compassion I had. There was no way to know what that person was going through. Why can't we just be honest and not say anything? A hug would go a lot further in these situations than trying to fill the air with insignificant chatter. Honestly saying, *"I don't know what to say,"* would be the best answer.

As the sun was setting, I rolled over to my back and looked up at the sky which was turning a dark red. Although anger was still simmering, my rage had subsided, and I began again with my illogical bargaining with God. I had reduced myself to someone who seemed to be trying to buy lemons from a street vendor in the marketplace; like a toddler trying to negotiate with his parents. All the bartering was useless, a single glove missing its match. Still no answers and the isolation oppressive as the sun dipped over the horizon and the night blanketed the island with a thick, almost tangible darkness.

My night was terrible; chasing after sleep the entire evening. At times catching it for a moment then as quickly, disappearing again. The waking hours were spent weeping, sobbing and re-living each moment that preceded Joanna's death. When I was able catch sleep, my dreams were full of vivid images of Death lurking in the shadows and beckoning me to join him. At times that seemed the easiest option.

As the sun peeked over the horizon the next morning, and many mornings after, I would wake to find myself emotionally chained on my knees in the path of those great waves, exhausted, unable to move, unable to escape, bound on the beach where they fell over and over, the glass shards snapping at my flesh. One after another they released their fury on me with no escape in sight; no remedy to be found. I felt forsaken, forgotten, hung out and left to "live" without hope.

Days had turned into weeks and what time not used to patch and re-build the shelter was spent devising a plan to get off the island. Some days I didn't want to escape the island and leave my sweet Joanna alone there. Other days, I was driven by something deep inside to break free. Still others, found me going through the motions from sunrise to sunset hoping the following day would be better.

On occasion I would still beat myself up over the whole situation too; wondering what I could have done differently or if my actions could have prevented any of this. Could I have saved her if I had not hesitated to throw the chair overboard? Should I have taken her to the ship's doctor when she first became sick? What if we had gone up to the main deck instead of our balcony that night? Countless questions with not one single answer. *"God, where are You?"* I wondered aloud.

Sitting on the beach the next day, staring out at the horizon, I noticed a large ship in the distance. This looked like the ship that Joanna and I had traveled on. "Can they see me?" I questioned aloud. Jumping to my feet, I began to flail my arms frantically as I ran along the beach trying desperately to attract attention to myself.

After a few long minutes, the boat slowly disappeared over the skyline. Did they see me? Were they sending help? Or was life just continuing without any concern for what I was faced with here on this stupid island? It appeared as if no one was looking for me or that no one even cared that I was here. Had they all given up on me?

Every few days or so, another ship passed by my quaint little island prison; some at night with the lights aglow with parties and dinner engagements, and the sound of music drifting across the waters toward me. Others, during the day with people carrying on their normal routines; the sound of children at play and laughter. I had built a signal fire, but no one seemed to notice. The fact that these ships continue on their respective courses gives the impression that life just continues out there without regard to my situation or what I am suffering here.

The little clams I had found on the beach along with a few coconuts here and there were the mainstays of my nutrition. The mussels were petite, but I was able to find enough of them to satisfy my hunger; plus, digging them kept me busy during the day. Keeping my mind occupied and my hands busy, helped the time pass without being completely consumed by my emotions.

Crabs were a mainstay in the community where we lived and quite a treat to be able to eat them. We loved them steamed, of course, and would enjoy them many times we went out to eat. Finding a few crabs one day, I was able to capture them and not having a pot to steam them in, resorted to just poking a stick through them and suspending them above the fire to cook. Although not as tasty as a steamed crab with all the spicy seasoning, it was comforting to eat something familiar.

I remembered one vacation Joanna and I had taken where we were able to scoop as many crabs up as we could with a little dip net as we walked along the beach. With the help of our children, our little five-gallon bucket was overflowing with the tasty crustaceans. We looked like two kids in a candy store as we ate to our hearts content that night at our little rental cabin. Since the kids didn't care for crab, they munched on PB&J sandwiches.

As I ate my crab meal that afternoon, I noticed a dark cloud out over the ocean with rain bands descending at a sharp angle from them. My mind went back to the great storm that caused me to end up on this island. I wondered if maybe someone else was out there on a ship and gripping the railing in fear; that possibly someone else was fighting for survival in the midst of the storm. For some reason, though, it didn't really matter to me. I didn't care about them. My situation was consuming me and my thoughts, and I didn't seem to have compassion for others.

Did I really think my situation was worse than anyone else going through a difficult time? I watched as the storm slowly moved eastward and out of sight and wrestled with these thoughts the entire time. A short time later, another ship passed by headed directly into the storm that had just disappeared. I wondered if the people on that ship knew what was lurking just over the horizon. I wondered if this storm would wreak havoc in someone's life. I wondered if anyone would warn them to take safety in the belly of the ship. I guess I wouldn't know unless some poor, unfortunate soul washed up on my beach.

As darkness overtook the island once again, the horizon lit up with bright flashes and I could hear the distant rumble of thunder.

Preparing myself for a rainstorm, I hunkered down inside my little shelter and waited for the rain. The storm arrived quickly, and the winds began to whip to the point of ripping the palm-branch-roof right off my shelter. Soon after, the rain began to fall. Raindrops the size of marbles pelted my location. The rain felt like needles on my skin and my clothing was soaked through in a matter of seconds.

The blackness of the night was interrupted every few seconds by great flashes of deadly lightning that illuminated everything around momentarily before darkness swallowed up the surroundings again. The storm was relentless. For several hours, the ice-cold rain on my skin had my teeth chattering like a monkey trying to get a date with a banana. Slowly, the storm moved off shore and the rain subsided. Everything was water-logged, and my fire had been extinguished.

As the sun came up the next day, I spent time spreading out my fire wood to dry and gathering up the palm fronds that had been blown away by the strong winds.

After patching up the shelter, a trip into the canopy was my next order of business. I had wanted to explore the sides of the mountain behind my location at the edge of the beach. Maybe a more suitable shelter location could be found to protect me from another storm like the one that had passed through the night before.

The rocks there were just as sharp, slippery and jagged as the ones I had climbed on that first day. Looking up the steep incline just below the cloud cover, I noticed a small opening in the rocks above me that could be a cave. An exploration of the cave was essential. This could be a place to weather any future storms that may come through the island.

Maybe another day would come, however, that I would want to explore it more closely. For now, the rocks and climb up would prove too difficult a challenge and strength was waning. My heart just didn't have the will to go up there that day. Some days I just wish I had died back there in the water with Joanna. At least we would still be together. As I looked up the side of the mountain, again wrestling with my thoughts, tears filled my eyes and I began to weep again. *"Can anyone help me?"* I heard myself sputter with tears streaming down my face.

8 THE GIFT BOX

The next day, almost as if someone heard my cries, I got quite the surprise. Out in the waters about halfway between the beach and the reefs, a small box was floating. Battling the waves at the shore briefly, I swam out to retrieve the box and bring it back to my shelter. It was a hard, plastic box comparable to one of those boxes musicians use to carry expensive equipment to a gig. Questions went off in my mind like a box of fireworks. What could be inside? Was it a treasure? Did it fall off one of those cruise ships that passed by? Was it from a drug deal gone bad. Was someone looking for it? Would I be in trouble for opening it? Was I in danger? I tucked the box inside my shelter and just sat and stared at it with my imagination running wild the entire time. I was like a kid at Christmas with an early package under the tree. It was around noon when my curiosity overtook me, and the suspense was more than I could handle. The box had to be opened.

Anticipation was at an all-time high as I twisted the latches on the box and slowly opened it up. Inside was a heavenly take-out meal from one of my favorite restaurants. The aroma inside tickled my nose and was reminiscent of walking into Grandma's house on Thanksgiving Day. The smell of good food had become almost foreign to me in the weeks since my landing here. The arrival of this box with food inside and the fragrance it offered was a welcomed addition to my little hut. The sustenance was just what I needed and was even still hot. The only regret was not opening it up sooner.

Barbeque ribs and roasted chicken with potato salad, collard greens, baked beans, and a big, fat yeast roll; a meal fit for a king. Sitting in the crude shelter, I consumed it like a dog that had been starved for days, given a fresh bone. The ribs were tender and delicious and bathed in my favorite sauce. The potato salad was certainly my Mom's recipe, and the collard greens had bits of ham in them making me think they were cooked with a ham hock. Not only food but some dry ice with bottled water and a grape soda, my favorite, in a separate compartment. After eating until my stomach ached, I began to wonder, *"Where did this box come from? Who did it belong to? Was it intended for me? If so, why don't they rescue me?"* Remembering my comment from yesterday I wondered, *"Is someone listening to me?"* These thoughts filled my mind as I lay there on my bed listening to the crackle of the dying fire. Such good news from the day and no one to share it with. Who would I be able to tell special things to now? Who would I be able to tell how my day went? Drifting off to sleep, I instinctively reached over to touch Joanna's hand. The reality of knowing she would never be there again caused me to cry myself to sleep.

The next morning found me sleeping longer than normal; probably because my stomach was full for the first time in a while. My body needed the rest and it was good finally catching up. Rubbing my eyes, I sat for a while considering the box that had arrived by sea the previous day. My face was wrapped in a slight grin thinking of the great food I had enjoyed the previous day. As I reflected, I picked up the box to look again to make sure I hadn't missed anything. A small scrap of folded paper that had gone unnoticed was tucked neatly in the bottom corner of the box. As the paper was unfolded, a scribbled message came to life. Scratched in a handwriting that seemed familiar, yet couldn't be placed, was a note that read: *"I know where you are. I want to help you. I really do care. But, you have to help me help you."* I dropped the note to my lap. *"What are they talking about?"* I wondered aloud. A quick scan of the horizon out across the reefs didn't reveal any ships waiting on the. Where was this person? Surely, if they could get a hot meal in here to me they could rescue me without me having to swim out to them. How was I able to wash up past the reefs onto the beach in the first place? How was Joanna's body able to show up on the shore? Preparing my mind for rescue, I began to wait to see if they would come. I scanned the horizon every day looking for a rescue ship; looking for anything that appeared to be coming for me.

Days had passed, and I was at a loss as to what I should do. Daily searches for additional gift boxes turned up nothing. No other boats besides the ones on the horizon that passed every few days oblivious to my presence. "Who is this that wants to rescue me?" I thought aloud. "What, exactly, do you need my help with?" I questioned with frustration in my voice.

The island felt as if it were closing in on me. The dark cloud that hovered overhead had been constant since I had been there. Maybe the ships passing on the horizon couldn't see the island because it was shrouded by that cloud. Plans were made to leave the island. If I could just get out past the coral reefs, then surely whoever it was could see me and take me to safety.

9 ATTEMPTED ESCAPE

Early the next day, my escape plan was in full swing. I fashioned a small raft out of the driftwood from my shelter and fastened it together with a few vines and pieces of t-shirt that I had torn into strips. The shirt had not been on my back much, plus, the sun was never going to shine here anyway it appeared. I fabricated a small paddle from the lid of the gift box and used my makeshift club as the handle.

Once the raft was latched together, I pushed it out into the breakers and began my exodus. The raft was handling the water pretty good and it looked as if my plan would be successful. I thought to myself, *"I'm about to be free from this island prison!"* The thought was short-lived, however, as I neared the edge of the reef. The waves were crashing in front of me forcefully. As the raft made its way up the face of the first wave, time seemed to freeze for a moment, and my mind went back to thoughts of Joanna. Thoughts of how I was unable to save her; her beautiful smile; the way she held my hand, her contagious laugh, her playing with the grandchildren.

As the waves pounded the reef, I saw, with slow-motion, liquid movement, each one rise from the ocean. On each wave face were memories, pictures, and glimpses of dreams. As each wave rose, the images and pictures would appear and disappear. Suddenly, they would turn black, buckle and shatter into cutting fragments that would become part of the beach as the waves tumbled toward the shoreline to make another deposit.

Abruptly, the waves in my face and ferocious force of the water brought me back to reality. The teeth of the salt water in my eyes blurred out any ability to see what was happening around me. All I knew to do was to hold on with all my might. Gripping the edges of the logs I felt the simple raft twist and shake then begin to disintegrate.

The poorly executed latching holding the raft together was no contender for the force of the waves. The next second I found myself in the water being agitated like I was inside a large washing machine with dirty, old razor blades and rusted barbed wire. As my body was tossed and thrown and grating across the coral below the surface, the intense bite of the salt water snapped at the fresh wounds like a chihuahua that didn't want to be coddled. The sections of the raft joined in the mugging as the logs waited in line to hammer my aching body with blunt force that took my breath away.

The ferocious waves launched me back toward the shore. Immediately the tremendous undertow would drag me back across the reef to begin the process again. The ebb and flow of the water had me trapped in its grip and I was losing flesh and blood with each cycle.

In the same way, the emotional wounds of losing Joanna once again were ripped open exposing the tender feelings again. At this exact moment, a decision had to be made. Should I quit fighting and let the water take me? Giving up would be easy. No more pain. No more sorrow. No more tears.

In my mind's eye, I saw a black vortex like a whirlpool opening just under the surface of the water. It was inviting me in. A darkness swirling and sucking the very remnants of hope from my heart. I could give in to the darkness or I could fight to survive.

Wave after wave tossed me back and forth like a volleyball in a heated match. As my head broke the surface of the water, gasping for air, I chose the latter. *"I want to live!"* I cried out. *"God, help me!"* I sputtered. Suddenly, it was as if someone grabbed me and snatched me from the grip of the surf and I found myself back in the slightly calmer waters of the lagoon. *"It's like this island does not want me to leave,"* I thought as I tried to swim toward the shore. The last of the waves swished me around in its mouth once more and spit me out onto the shore. Banged up, battered, bleeding, and bruised, I crawled on hands and knees back to the edge of the canopy to nurse my wounds. I just sat for a while staring at the waves, emotionless and empty wondering what I was doing here and considering what had happened out there on the reef.

Sitting on the beach and looking eastward, dark clouds were forming on the horizon. Remembering that my shelter was now a destroyed raft, I made the decision to venture up the side of the cliff to find out if there was shelter in the cave I noticed a few weeks back. Getting stuck out here in another storm without shelter was a venture that I would avoid at all costs.

With my hands and feet wrapped in large leaves and not certain of their effectiveness, I began my ascent to the cave. Although it was not too far up, it felt like an eternity. I navigated the sharp jagged rocks with minimal injuries but still bleeding, nonetheless.

Approaching the small cave opening, I wondered what could be inside. Maybe a bear was hibernating in there. *"Wayne. Really? A bear?"* I heard myself ask. With much reluctance, I stuck my head inside the entrance and allowed my eyes to adjust to the darkness. After a few moments, it became apparent that the cavern was larger than anticipated. Slivers of light coming through from cracks in the rocks above offered more illumination than I would have thought. As my eyes became accustomed to the darkness, I saw something that took my breath away. Was someone here?

10 THE CAVE

Near the center of the cave was a crude table made from what looked like an old shipping crate. Cups and bowls made from coconut shells rested peacefully on the table as if they had just been used. In the darkness I could also see a couple of stumps that appeared to have been fashioned into simple chairs. To the right side of the cave was a large depression in the rock where rainwater collected. In the back of the cavern was a vertical wall that was flat and coated with a substance that reminded me of an old school chalkboard.

The manner in which the light shone through from above illuminated this wall as if it were beckoning me to come closer. Between me and the wall, there was a small fire pit with partially burned wood and ashes from a long-forgotten fire. Unconsciously, I reached down to feel if there was any warmth to make sure it was as old as I assumed.

The entire wall in front of me, floor to ceiling, was covered in etchings and writings. Some of these writings were written with some sort of chalk and others were etched into the surface of the stone. There were messages and notes from other people who had been on this island before me; hundreds of them.

Instinctively, I called out, *"Helloo? Anyone here?"* Nothing. Just the echoes of my own voice and then complete silence again. Looking around, I began to read some of the etchings. Guilt tried to overtake me like I was sneaking a peek at someone's diary but was compelled to continue.

Some of the carvings were dated and read like a journal entry or diary. Others seemed to be random thoughts. Although I had been on this island a few months already, I was truly discouraged when I read that someone named Elizabeth had been on this island back in the 1970s for over 18 years before she was able to leave. Still, I'm not certain if she was rescued or not.

Another man, Carl, had etchings over the course of two years that were undated. Still another man was on the island for only six months. Countless writings covered the wall.

As I looked at all the inscriptions, tons of questions zipped through my mind. Why were they here? How did these people escape the island? How were they rescued? Are any of them still here? Maybe someone left a clue in their messages as to how I could escape the grip of an island that seemed claustrophobic and squeezing the life out of me.

The collection of imprints in the cave wall were almost unlimited and I sat and read until the sun began to fade and I lost the ability to see the wall clearly. One thing seemed certain from what I've had seen so far, all these people were in similar situations as myself. All of them going about their daily lives and the loss of someone they loved catapulted them somehow to this small island.

As daylight faded, I rushed back down to the beach to my former shelter and picked up a few pieces of firewood and scooped up a couple of warm coals with a piece of bamboo. Making my way back inside the cave, I spent a little time starting a fire in the "fireplace." Settling in with my thoughts, I began to try and make some kind of sense out of my new-found shelter and the mysteries I had uncovered.

Laying in my new surroundings that night, the sun could not come up soon enough for me to be able to read some more of these writings and maybe discover a hint as to how to get my backside off Alcatraz. There were certainly mysteries here that needed to be unraveled. As I lay in the darkness of the cave with the light of the fire dancing on the walls around me, I wondered if maybe one of the people who had written on this wall in the past was the same person who sent the care package earlier. What they needed my help with, I still don't know. Hopefully I will find the answer tomorrow. These thoughts ran through my head until consciousness finally relented to exhaustion and I fell sound asleep.

11 WRITINGS ON THE WALL

As soon as the sun offered enough light in the cave the next morning, I was standing at the wall reading again. There were some especially interesting stories there, but, I was drawn to one in particular. The lady, Elizabeth, whose story I had been reading on the wall, seemed like a super-nice lady. Piecing together her thoughts made me wonder what happened to her after she was able to get off the island. It seems she and her husband had a wonderful relationship; similar to Joanna's and mine. They had been married almost fifty years when cancer took her husband away, but, how she wound up there in that cave was not clear.

She had many daily entries on the wall and was faithful to document her days religiously. Some days she had written long paragraphs where she was re-living certain life events and some days, nothing but a simple sentence with no definite emotion tied to it. It did seem as if she got to the point she enjoyed staying on the island.

She talked of setting up house there and going about her daily activities hoping no one would disturb her time. She seemed to be self-absorbed with her loss and was content to be in mourning until she died. It's almost as if she wanted to stay there all that time. It looked like she just embraced her loss and situation and just lived in mourning the rest of her time. She wrote of an elderly man who visited her on occasion but she would not let him stay for very long each time he visited. She wrote that he stopped coming by after a while and she was glad that she didn't have to deal with entertaining him.

Her diary entries were filled with bouts of crying and sadness on most days and the writings just end abruptly. I'm not sure if she didn't just die on the island. I could certainly understand if she did. Her writings made me wonder.

One thing she wrote, *"I've discovered something here. You don't lose someone all at once. You lose them in small pieces over time."* This struck a chord in my soul. I realized that if you lost someone all at once, then the healing process could start at that precise moment and be over sooner. But when it happens in little chunks here and there, it's like pulling a scab from a wound every time it begins to heal. Each time the pain is equal to or worse than the initial injury. Even so, no matter how many times or how few times the scab gets ripped off, there will always be that scar, always be that aching void.

Each time I remembered something about Joanna; her smile, her unique laugh, her encouragement; a scab got snatched off and I found myself tender and hurting like I had just lost her for the first time again. I understood what Elizabeth was feeling for sure. They say a picture paints a thousand words; I would say a shattered picture produces a thousand fragments.

The way the pictures and memories appeared on the face of the waves and shattered makes complete sense now. Each time, losing a small piece of the life we once shared. Each remnant cutting again and bringing more pain.

Earl, whose handwriting appeared to have been scratched on the wall in a fury, had lost a son. His writings detailed how much he loved his son and that he was taken away in the prime of his life. From his diary entries, it is apparent that his son was lost in a war; I assumed it was World War II from the dates. Maybe it was D-day on the beaches of Normandy. Who knows?

He was heartbroken that his dreams and visions for his own son were terminated before they could be realized. He, too, talked about an old man who came to visit while he was in the cave. Earl would have nothing to do with this visitor and actually wrote about cussing him out and making him leave. This man never really got over the loss of his son and he still blamed God years after the fact.

From his writings, I wasn't convinced that Earl didn't end his own life. He had so much life ahead of him but seemed he was determined in his mind he could not escape the island any other way. This made me sad. I stopped reading for a while and went out to the entrance of the cave to sit and contemplate what I had been reading.

From this vantage point, the breakers at the reef. seemed to be daring me to try to escape again. Rubbing my wounds that were healing but still aching, I succumbed to the fact that I was afraid to try that again; it was just too painful. The waves won the battle that day.

I looked down to where my shelter had been on the beach and my mind wandered back a few days to when I had gone through a fit of rage on the beach. I could relate to Earl's anger. After thinking back on my outburst, I felt compelled to apologize to God.

My emotions burst like an earthen dam as the words came off my tongue and I became a blubbering mess. Nothing humanly intelligible came from my mouth but I know God understood exactly what I was trying to say. He honors true repentance, I believe, and after my conversation with him, the weight of the guilt from that whole scenario was gone.

I wondered what the J.J. stood for in his writings; Maybe James John or Joe Jefferson but his writings were signed J.J. Banks. J.J. wrote extensively about the guilt of his loss. He lost his mom in an automobile accident and it seems J.J. was driving the car. The family was on a vacation and he recounts how he should have stopped for gas earlier instead of waiting. The rest stop would have been faster if they had stopped there instead of going on toward a gas station for a pit stop.

All the things he should have done or could have done were placing tremendous guilt on him. It seems someone driving the other direction had fallen asleep at the wheel and came across the median and hit his car spinning it like a top.

Everyone was banged up and bruised but the impact was too much for his mother who was older and her body too frail for such trauma. She was alive for a short while at the scene but was pronounced dead when she arrived at the hospital.

J.J. wrote that surely he could have performed CPR or something to help. If only he had done more; if only he had done less; if only he had done something else, his mom would possibly still be with them. His writings were filled with the "if only" statements.

My mind went back to the night Joanna fell overboard. If only I had jumped in sooner. If only I had thrown over a life ring. If only I had notified the ship's captain. If only I had prayed harder. Countless "if only" questions inundated my mind and I could completely understand the guilt that J.J. was going through.

J.J. wrote about a friend named Andy that visited him on the island and through lengthy discussions and long evenings talking through the situation, came to the understanding that it was not J.J.'s fault that his mother was gone. J.J. wrote about how liberated he felt once he came to that conclusion and quit blaming himself for the loss of his mother.

How were all these visitors getting to this island? It seems almost every wall entry has mention of an old man, a Grandpa, Andy or someone who visits with them. Who were these people and why hasn't anyone visited me? I could use a little conversation at least.

J.J. recalled the precious memories of his mom with tenderness and spoke of the legacy she left with not only him but with his wife and children. He also talked about climbing the mountain on his way off the island. Hmmm?

The next few weeks were mind numbing; reading the wall, trying to put myself in each one's shoes and then trying to make sense of what I had read. Surely there was a clue hidden in these writings. Each one was similar but completely different. Some long; some short. Some infinitely descriptive; some vague. I was certain of one thing; I was completely alone on this island. All these people were able to leave somehow. But how.

There was a lot of talk in the etchings about time spent on the beach. Maybe I should get back down to the beach and see if there were clues there not previously discovered. I didn't relish the thought of walking along that shoreline. Even in flip flops, the tiny fragments would nip at my feet and leave me in so much pain that it made me want to stay in the shelter of my little cave. But, I had to go down there and try to make sense of things. The decision was made to spend some time there to see if I could decipher the puzzles from what I had been reading.

Walking along the beach one of those days, I took special notice of all the glass shards along the shoreline. Each one, fragments of the life I had once shared with Joanna. I reached down and picked one up to examine it more closely. The constant pounding of the waves had made the edges of the shard smooth. It was still sharp and jagged but not as razor sharp as it was the first day it was deposited there. It reminded me of sea glass.

If I were in one of those tourist-laden places, these would be scarfed up in a moment. But here, I could enjoy them without the plunder of others. I sat down at the water's edge and picked up a few pieces and admired their colors and shapes.

As the water licked at my toes, I saw a rather large fragment and admired the intricate details and the prominent painting on the top. I remembered fondly Joanna's and my trips along the beach with our necks bent forward in the "tourist" posture. We called it the "tourist" posture because that's the way all of the "out of towners" looked while searching for sea shells or sea glass along the waterfront.

Oblivious to our surroundings, we would walk along looking for that prized sand dollar until we came to our senses and realized we looked just like the "tourists." Laughing at ourselves, we would look back over our shoulders to see how far we had wandered, make a U-turn and trace our steps over again back to our starting point. I chuckled to myself and tossed the fragment back into the waves and watched as it rolled and receded with each wave that rose and broke on the beach. As I did, I noticed a small cut on my hand. Another loss. More pain.

Late that afternoon, I climbed back up the mountain to take refuge in the cave. Every time I was in the cave, I was drawn to the wall and its words. A small writing in the lower right corner of the wall captured my attention; brief, but intentional and may have been the first clue I had come across. It read, *"I've discovered it is impossible to leave the island the same way you came."* I chuckled aloud and under my breath said, *"You got that right buddy,"* wishing I had seen this prior to my escape attempt. The writing continued, *"You can't go back via the sea. You gotta climb the mountain and get above the clouds." "Climb the mountain?"* I heard myself ask aloud, *"Is that even possible?"*

My words echoed around the cave for a moment before returning to my ears. The mountain was high and steep; the rocks sharp and jagged. What was even up there? The smoky-gray fog that hung ominously above gave me no glimpse of anything above it. I wasn't even sure how tall this mountain was. Where would I go once I reached the top? What would I do; flag down an airplane? This was a ridiculous notion and I would have no part of climbing that hellacious mountain. It would be too difficult, plus, my will to attempt such a feat had vacated the premises. My mind wandered as I scanned the wall some more.

As I skimmed across the writings, I found one etched in an early elementary handwriting style. Her name was Maggie and she seemed to have lost her parents. She was only 6 years old at the time. Her stay here was short, and she talked about "Grandpa" joining her here but not her "real Grandpa". It seemed another person was here with her and she spoke fondly of this "old man" who helped her navigate her escape from the island.

She talked about how he shared his ice cream with her and how he held her hand as they walked down the beach together picking up pieces of sea glass. *"Who was this old man?"* I asked myself. There was a mosaic in the shape of a cross made from sea glass I assume

Maggie had made with the help of this Grandpa fellow; crude but uniquely beautiful at the same time. Looking at it reminded me of some of the crafts my own children had brought home from Sunday School when they were younger and hung on our refrigerator for weeks.

As I lay down that evening with thoughts of this "Grandpa" in my mind. I wondered who that man was and how he ended up here with that little girl. I also wondered where he found ice cream on this island. What I wouldn't give for a bite of an ice cream sandwich right about now. I would discover answers to these questions sooner than I anticipated.

DOUG JOHNSON

12 THE VISITOR

Early the next morning, as I sat in the cave, staring at the writing wall, I could hear the crackle of the fire and feel the warmth of its glow on my face. The rising sun introduced the slivers of light once again into my new little home. There was something comforting about this place. Maybe it was the way the sunlight shone in through the cracks above or the way the light from the fire danced happily on the wall. The fact that I was sharing experiences of others through their writings was reassuring somehow and I didn't feel as lonely as before.

Maybe I would just stay here forever I thought. The peaceful silence of that thought was suddenly shattered. *"How's it going?"* I heard from behind me and to my left. My head was spinning, and fear gripped me at the same time. Surely, I was going insane. I had not heard another voice in some time but was certain of what I had just heard. *"Who could this be?"* I wondered.

I jumped to my feet and wheeled around quickly toward the voice I heard and saw an elderly gentleman sitting on one of the stump chairs. His legs were crossed, and his faded old pants revealed their age with stains and areas where the fabric was thinning and frayed slightly. You could tell he was a working man just from his clothing. His face was weathered and the lines and wrinkles read like a roadmap of experience. He was sporting probably a three-day beard growth and his old plaid shirt reminded me of what I thought lumberjacks to wear. The tufts of white hair were mussed and tucked under an old floppy fishing hat. You know, the kind of hat with fishing lures attached around the brim.

I struggled to catch my breath but heard myself say instinctively, *"Fine. And you?"* What was I thinking? I was not fine. Plus, I had a ton of questions to ask. I stammered, *"Who wh.. who are you? How, How did you get in here? Why are you here? What, wh... what..."* *"Hold on young man,"* the man continued, *"that's a lot of questions. First, my name is Andy, but most folks just call me Grandpa."* *"What's your name, fella?"*

I know I should have been alarmed with this situation but something about his demeanor and his voice was calming to me. He was eerily familiar, yet I was certain we had never met. His deep blue eyes sparkled like the sea when first illuminated by the rays of the morning sun. He just looked at me over the tiny wire-framed glasses that had slid down to the tip of his nose. It was almost as if he knew what I was thinking before I said anything; and those eyes pierced my soul but not in a way that I felt he was judging me. It was more of a reassurance that he wanted me to know he was concerned about my well-being and just wanted to help.

I wondered if this was the same Grandpa the little girl, Maggie, had encountered. Maybe he could tell me how to get off the island. Maybe he held the keys to what I had been looking for. *"My name is Wayne,"* I replied quickly. *"How do I get off this island?"* I heard myself blurt out again. Grandpa just chuckled, *"Heh, heh, heh. You don't care much for small talk, do you son? It's a pleasure to make your acquaintance, Wayne."* He stated rather simply. *"How... how long have you been here?"* I stammered. *"Oh, I've been around for a while,"* said Grandpa. *"What do you mean?"* I asked. *"Where have you been and why haven't I seen you before now? Have you been hiding from me?"* Grandpa just smiled and picked up a stick and began to poke the fire.

I had a million questions, but Grandpa seemed to be in no hurry to answer them. I got the impression that I wasn't going to get answers to my questions right away, so we just made small talk for a while. Grandpa pulled an apple out of his pocket and with the other hand, a pocket knife. After peeling it, he sliced it and offered me a slice. As I reached out to take it from him, his eyes met mine and he reassured me with a slight wink and said, *"Apples are a lot better for you than ice cream sandwiches."* How did he know what I was thinking last night?

As I bit into the apple, the sweet juice squirted out and began to run down my chin. Wiping my face with my arm, I realized I hadn't enjoyed a piece of fruit this tasty in a very long time. Instinctively, I reached out for another slice and Grandpa was kind enough to oblige. We continued until the entire apple was devoured.

We talked about the weather and the storm that originally brought me to the island. We talked about family and Joanna. He asked about our children and grandchildren like he knew them personally. I responded with the customary, *"They are fine,"* not really knowing otherwise or how they were coping with Joanna and I both being gone right then. We carried on for a couple of hours with Grandpa leading the visit by asking questions of me. Although my mind was still searching for answers, my heart was satisfied. Since I had no questions for him that he seemed to want to answer, the conversation waned to the point of being awkward.

It was akin to being at one of those dinner parties you have been invited to by a friend of a friend and you must carry on conversations with different ones that you don't know for an entire evening.

This has always been difficult for me. Even working in real estate for so many years, I hated those networking events that you had to go to on occasion and "work the room." This was where I really missed Joanna. If she were there, I could have looked to her with that "I'm out of words" stare and she would have taken over and carried the conversation. Not in an overbearing way but in a way that supported me. That's just the way she was; graceful and elegant.

Meanwhile, the awkward silence didn't seem to bother the old man. He was just as relaxed as a full opossum under anesthesia in the noon-day sun. His expression never changed; smiling like he had just awakened from a happy dream. We just stared at each other for a few uncomfortable moments. Well, he was staring at me and my eyes were darting back and forth like a sparrow who was being chased by a hawk without a place to land.

13 CLEAR VISION

"Do you like fishing? Why don't we go fishing, Wayne?" Grandpa asked. *"Fishing? How can we go fishing at a time like this?"* I wondered to myself. Before I could make an objection, I noticed that Grandpa already had a couple of rods and reels in his hand with a small tackle box. *"Where did he have these hidden?"* I wondered. This was all not making sense to me. I wasn't sure that this wasn't just a dream. I took my thumb and forefinger and pinched myself on the arm. The pain of the pinch told me immediately that it was not a dream and indeed happening.

For an older man, Grandpa was uncommonly nimble and was able to make his way down the side of the hill with the agility of a mountain goat. Almost like he had done it many times before. I, on the other hand, took a little more time to navigate the rocks trying my best to protect my hands and feet from further damage.

Once I reached Grandpa's side, my pole was already rigged and waiting for me. Grandpa made a cast out into the surf and within seconds was pulling a large fish to the beach. I cast my line into the water and waited patiently with no tug on my line whatsoever. I watched as Grandpa pulled in yet another fish. I tried to copy what he was doing but didn't seem to have the knack for it like he did.

We fished for half the day and I was not able to land a single thing. Grandpa caught several more and released them once he got them to shore. He finally put down his rod and came over to me to give me some pointers on what I was doing wrong. The only comment I can remember was when he jokingly said, *"You're not holding your mouth right."* We both laughed. My very next cast, however, I hooked a really nice fish and was able to bring it to shore. Grandpa just beamed and grinned like a dad who just watched his son hit a walk-off homerun in a championship baseball game.

"It wasn't your fault, you know," Grandpa said calmly. *"What?"* I questioned. *"Joanna. Her accident. It wasn't your fault,"* he said. I just stared for a moment before realizing my eyes had begun to tear up. As tears began to run

down my cheeks, I was able to muster, *"Thanks. I needed to hear that."* I had already come to this conclusion after reading J.J.'s wall writings but to hear it from someone else reaffirmed my confidence that I had done all I could do to save Joanna that fateful night.

I liked this guy. There was something comforting about being with him. He seemed genuinely interested in me and seemed to have compassion for what I was going through. I had lost both of my Grandfathers at an early age and never really had a relationship like this in my life. I remembered thinking that this must be what it was like to have a Grandfather.

We took the fish we kept and tackle with us and made our way back up to the confines of the cave. Grandpa stoked the fire and used a straight stick for a makeshift shish-kabob. It seemed he had a knack for taking something insignificant and turning it into something useful in his hands. He cooked the fish to perfection and we ate until our bellies were swollen like a young puppy who has just been given a big bowl of warm milk.

As we sat by the fire, I felt contentment for the first time in a long time. I felt as if, for a fleeting moment, things were going to be okay. Glancing over at the wall, a writing I had never seen before caught my eye. It read, *"God said,*

'Everything's going to be okay.' He's got this." I looked over at Grandpa and he was busy with his tackle box and making sure the rods were ready for the next outing. I thought to myself that I wasn't sure if God would have anything to do with me after the way I treated him earlier in my stay here. I was embarrassed just thinking about that tirade on the beach.

I wondered if Grandpa had seen me having that fit. If so, he had not mentioned it but, somehow, I was sure he did. Without thinking, I just blurted out, *"I'm sorry for being so angry the other day. I hope that I didn't offend you."* Grandpa just smiled reaffirming what I had already felt. *"I don't recall you being angry,"* Grandpa said. If he did see my outburst on the beach, it seemed as if he genuinely had forgotten it. There was something liberating about just confessing that to someone else though. It was as if a beached whale had been lifted off me and I could breathe again. I took a deep breath.

After staring at the fire for a while, I got up and made my way over to the cave's entrance. As I stood there looking down toward the beach below, I felt Grandpa beside me. He had walked up and was looking down just as I was. *"What're you looking at?"* He questioned as he put his arm around my shoulders. *"Nothing,"* was my emotionless answer. *"Here, put these on,"* Grandpa said. I looked over and he had pulled his glasses off and had them in his hand extended toward me. My first reaction was to reject his offer completely. He had a look on his face reminiscent of a gift-giver waiting with anticipation for the recipient to open the gift they had just delivered. Without much more thought, I took the glasses and slipped them onto my face. *"There. That ought to do it,"* Grandpa chuckled as he walked back toward the fire pit.

Looking around, it was as if this prescription was exactly what I needed for my eyes. Taking in everything in the cave, my vision was crystal clear and the details astonishing. The fire in the fireplace came alive as the flames danced the salsa. The writing wall was vivid and vibrant. Even the rudimentary furnishings looked as if from a showroom catalog. As I turned and looked back down to the beach below, I was not prepared for what my eyes would behold.

DOUG JOHNSON

14 NOT ALONE

As I gazed to the beach below, I saw hundreds of people in the shards of shattered dreams and memories facing out toward the ocean crying in despair. I watched as some cried on their knees and others in fetal positions just groaning in anguish. Still others in a fit of rage that looked all too familiar to the display that I had made a few weeks earlier. It appeared that each of them were unaware that the others were there.

I turned around quickly to Grandpa and asked, *"Where did all these people come from?"* Grandpa just looked at me with a solemn stare and said rather bluntly, *"They have been here all along."* *"What? No! I have been here alone all this time,"* I shouted. *"None of these people were here!"* I turned back to the beach. Taking a closer look, I began to notice familiar faces on the beach. Faces of friends, family members, even our children and grandchildren, each one mourning the loss of Joanna in their own way. What did this mean? How had I not been able to see it? How did they get here?

Grandpa came over to me and put his arm around my shoulders. *"Son, you couldn't see them because you were only focused on yourself and your personal pain. You see, each one of these people lost Joanna too. Each one is mourning her loss in different ways. They all need for you to show them the way off the island."* "But," I objected, *"I don't know how to get off this island. I'm stranded here!"* "Yes, you do son," He replied gently. *"You must climb the mountain. It will be painful, and you may fall, but, I will go with you and you can do it."*

I was finally beginning to understand what I was missing. I was so in tune with myself and had closed out everyone else that I believed I was the only one hurting, the only one going through misery, the only one experiencing a loss. Somehow, I was the key to helping everyone around me find the way off the island. All of a sudden, I had this confidence deep in my soul that God was in control and through every trial and storm He would never let me go. His grace was sufficient for whatever I was going through. I grabbed Grandpa and pulled him in close and hugged him tightly.

I spent a great deal of time on that beach with my family and friends talking, remembering, and crying. Taking moments with each one and letting them all process their pain in the ways they felt best. But, I eventually made the decision to climb the black jagged cliffs up through the clouds and away from the waves of crushed memories and dreams. I gathered all those along the shore who were willing and told them it was time to climb.

DOUG JOHNSON

15 THE MOUNTAIN

The trek up the mountain was harder than I expected. Several times we lost our footing and would slide back down a way before we could gather ourselves and begin to climb again. Every time I thought we couldn't go any further, I would look up and see Grandpa. He would shout things like, *"Come on! You can do it!"* He was constantly cheering us all to come up where he was.

There were times we had to stop climbing and rest for the mountainside was steep and the rocks painful. After a time of rest, we would begin the slow climb again; every day getting closer and closer to the top. Each time, Grandpa just above calling us up to himself. Occasionally throwing down a rope to assist with our climb or climbing down and helping to carry us over some obstacle in our way.

Some days, one of those in our group would lose their footing and slide all the way back down to the beach. A few of our company would go back down to the beach to help them get back up to where the rest of the troupe waited. Each one waiting would mimic Grandpa's encouragement in their own ways. This would continue until the all the climbers were reunited again. Our focus would then turn upward to the mountaintop and we would begin to scale again.

It seemed as if we were on the side of the mountain for some time and the ascent was not an easy one. But, once our heads finally broke through the top of the clouds and the sun shone on our faces for the first time in ages, I wept; not tears of sorrow but of joy. I had missed the sunlight more than I had realized. The gray and murky skies were replaced by brilliant light. I looked around only to realize that we were once again back on the cruise ship and that we were surrounded by our friends and loved ones who had made the trip as well.

There was a lot of hugging and laughter. Now, we recounted our memories with joy instead of sorrow and shared, with fondness, stories of Joanna and her enjoyment of this infinitely temporal life. I found myself belly-laughing at one point. I finally had hope for good things for my future. I drew in a deep breath and now realized I could finally breathe again.

Making my way back to the cabin, uncertain of how my emotions would respond, my walk was resolute to face the fears before me. Pausing briefly, with my hand on the doorknob, I twisted the latch and let the door swing open on its own.

Looking inside, the flood of memories overcame me like a tidal wave. I could feel my eyes tearing up and then drop after drop they wet my cheeks and fell helplessly to the floor. Her toothbrush in the stand, her pajamas on the chair, her shoes neatly tucked under the edge of the bed. She was everywhere, and she was nowhere.

Turning to sit on the edge of the bed my eyes wandered to the balcony. Thoughts of that fateful night collided with my mind and heart like a freight train out of control. I could recall with vivid detail her doubling over in pain and flipping over the railing to the water below.

My body collapsed, and I fell backward on the bed with uncontrollable sobs. Rolling over to my stomach I buried my face in one of the pillows nearby. The scent of Joanna on the pillow hit my nose and another avalanche of emotion came tumbling down. All other sound was silenced by my distressful cries.

When the crying began to wane, my ears became tuned to a familiar sound. I could hear waves breaking on a beach again. As I cracked open my eyes to peer through tear-soaked eyes, I found myself back on the beach again, face down in the sand. New shards, new slivers of memories all around, razor sharp, and I was bleeding from the fresh cuts once again.

Looking up at the mountain, I knew what I must do. I spent a few moments on the beach before beginning the climb again. Grandpa met me on the beach and spoke many words of encouragement. He had said he believed in me and stayed with me all the way back up the mountain.

Over the years, I would find myself on the beach on occasion and then climb again; faster each time. Each time a little less painful; each time a little easier.

A lot of time has passed since the event that broke my heart in ways I never imagined. This one event tossed me, first, into a sea of sorrow, then chained me in the path of its relentless pounding on an island called grief. It changed me. It changed my view of life. It changed my belief system.

I still go back to the beach on occasions; days like today. Today was Joanna's birthday. As I look back down from the climb up, I realize the greatest disappointments in life always follow the greatest expectations. Truth is, I had great expectations for life, perhaps expecting to live a fairy-tale existence without tragedy, without loss, with family and friends I adore, co-workers I cherish and the forever endless sharpening that one human being gives to another.

So, as I miss what I had and what I thought to be, I appreciate what now is and who God has allowed to stay and who God has allowed to come into my life. I have discovered that to love deeply is not a sin, to dream big is not a sin, to grieve intensely is not a sin, nor is it a sin to love again, or dream again. The sun is up, and color has returned to my life and the guilt of living, indeed of loving, is diminished. The fear to taste joy is burned off like a fog, revealing the beauty that remains. For the darkness of the loss here is illuminated by the promise of the other side, where shadow and tear find no place, and the voices from the past sing and laugh in endless joy, where all things are made new.

DOUG JOHNSON

****

AUTHOR'S ENCOURAGEMENT

This story, although fictional, relates to anyone who is going through grief and the loss of a loved one. I, too, lost my wife, Patty, to a four-year battle with breast cancer after nearly thirty-five years of marriage.

As a part of humanity, we all have many things in common. One of those things is the loss of a loved one. Have you ever wondered why it seems some go through difficult times and others do not? Have you ever felt as if you, too, were alone on an island of struggle with thoughts full of questions? Have you ever declared, "Life isn't fair!"?

There is not a day that goes by that I don't think of her or cherish a memory that comes to my mind. So, I know the pain of losing someone close; of losing a best friend. I just wanted the pain to go away. I wanted it to stop hurting so badly. First, let me say that all the events of Patty's passing did not take God by surprise. It didn't knock Him off His throne and He was not wringing His hands wondering what He was going to do with me now. Somehow, this has been a part of His plan for my life from the day I was born. Do I understand it? No. Do I trust Him? Absolutely!

Now, here you stand in the cave staring at my writings on the wall. Possibly you are navigating through a loss. I want you to know, first, you're not alone. Throngs of people have stood where you are standing today. No one is exempt from loss during their lifetime. Christ-followers, and even Jesus Himself, experienced this deep sense of loss.

Jesus tells us in John 16:33, *"I have said these things to you, that in me you may have peace. In the world you will have tribulation. But take heart; I have overcome the world."* Here is what you need to understand from the beginning; we will all face trials and tribulations. If you are a believer, however, you can expect to come through this time victoriously. That's right. God will bring His people through every difficult season. He has a plan for your life and it's a good plan. Even though our lives are in tumult now, God will bring everything together and make it good again.

When I lost Patty, I scoured the internet searching for a plan or some type of program to help me walk through the valley I found myself in. I supposed if there were certain steps to take, that I could just get on the fast track and accomplish each step to get myself off that island more quickly.

Here's the bad news. There is no single system nor a twelve-step plan to navigate you through this journey, but, know that there is a way out; there is hope. Now, there are specific stages or symptoms of grief, but, each person arrives at and leaves each of these stages in a random order and doesn't experience each one necessarily. These feelings are common, and you are not weird if you find yourself crying constantly or if you feel guilt that somehow you could have prevented the events that catapulted you here. If you are experiencing a loss right now, the last thing you want to hear is that it takes time. But, it does.

You're not going to figure out how you will get through this season with your natural mind. I tried so many times to try and see the end from the beginning. It is a day by day journey and God doesn't reveal His entire life plan for us all at once. Just see the next step and take them one at a time. You may consider speaking with a grief counselor or a pastor. It helps to verbalize what you are going through.

If you do, please go to someone who is grounded in the Bible, the word of truth. It does help to get your thoughts out and let someone be a sounding board for you even if it's a close friend or relative. The best counsellor you can employ at this time, however, is the Great Comforter, the Holy Spirit.

Don't listen to counsel from anyone with information that is contrary to what God's word says. Psalm 146:5 says, *"Do not put your trust in princes, in human beings, who cannot save."* The enemy of your soul wants to deceive you and uses unfair tactics to do so. His only goal is to steal, kill and destroy your life. There are well-meaning people, even family members and friends, who just want to help but their words are sometimes misdirected. Don't give in to the devil's lies or think that God doesn't care about you. God does love you more than you can imagine and wants the extreme best for you. You are not alone.

I know from personal experience what a deep loss feels like. And, although everyone processes things differently, it was still an extremely painful and an emotional process. It is okay to grieve. It is okay to cry. Shock and denial are common. I went from infinitely emotional lows to highs and even laughed at some points early on. There were days I thought Patty would walk through the door and I would wake up from a terrible dream. There were days I was in denial not believing that she was really gone. I would call her voicemail to hear her voice but hang up before I could leave a message. I was in shock that God would allow her to die after she and I had prayed vigilantly for her healing. These feelings are normal, and it is not a sin to hurt and feel hurt.

Maybe you have guilt that you could have done something differently to change the outcome of the situation. Maybe your actions or lack of action make you feel responsible somehow. Again, your enemy uses our emotions to our demise. Trust and hope in your Heavenly Father and do not succumb to the lies of the devil. Psalm 146 continues in verses 5-10, *"Blessed are those whose help is the God of Jacob, whose hope is in the Lord their God. He is the maker of heaven and earth, the sea, and everything in them—he remains faithful forever. He upholds the cause of the oppressed and gives food to the hungry. The Lord sets prisoners free, the Lord gives sight to the blind, the Lord lifts up those who are bowed down, the Lord loves the righteous. The Lord watches over the foreigner and sustains the fatherless and the widow, but he frustrates the ways of the wicked. The Lord reigns forever, your God, O Zion, for all generations. Praise the Lord."*

I remember feeling guilty for laughing only weeks after Patty had died. Pain and guilt can be expected. Since everyone processes things differently, I couldn't feel guilty about laughing and moving forward with my life. Proverbs 17:22 tells us, *"A merry heart does good like a medicine."* I couldn't think others were crass if they remembered Patty and laughed at memories they had. They were on the beach too, and each one climbed the mountain the best way they knew how.

Maybe you have lost someone you love and that is why you are reading this book right now. Maybe you, too, are on that beach right now with the waves of sorrow throwing remnants of a life that once was on the beach in the form of shattered dreams and memories.

Although your loved one is gone, life continues forward. The earth still turns on its axis and you must move with it or else you, too, will get stuck on this island. Everyone who has experienced a loss like this visits this island. It is not a place you want to set up camp and stay forever. Know that the Lord promises us that he sustains the widow and the fatherless. I believe this scripture could also include any loss of family; mother, father, sister, brother, child. God Himself will lift you up. Let God help you begin the climb. How long you stay on the island is totally up to you.

The ship in this story is representative of our life's journey. We get married, start a family, work at jobs or at home while not knowing where our lives will go or where we will end up. How many of us would actually sign up for a cruise not knowing where the ship was going? But, in life, we all sign on with great expectations of how it will end and the places we will go. Of course, we all want the fairy tale that ends, "and they lived happily ever after." But, that is exactly what that is; a fairy tale. There are no "happily ever afters" here on this earth. The Bible tells us in Hebrews 9:27, *"It is appointed unto man once to die."* So, our hopes are tied to a heavenly home instead where, truly, our joy will be everlasting.

We live in a fallen world and we are confronted with the storms of life every day. We must not lose sight that we are in a battle for eternity and must look at it this way. In our battles, we fight as individuals. God brings others alongside, to help us, train us, and hone our skills. Some of these people are here for our entire lives; others only a short time and we lose them. These losses can either make us useless in this battle or they can strengthen our mettle and resolve to finish our own course with honor and be worthy of the commendation, "Job well done! Enter into the joy of the Lord." How we fight is ours alone.

We cannot win the battle tagging along on the coat tail of another. Fight the good fight.

Along our journey, questions will come and go. What was the purpose for this pain? Did I weep for nothing? I do not believe it a sin to ask questions. But, we must begin to ask another type of question that is ultimately hard for most of us to ask. God, what can I learn from this experience? How can this help me in my relationship with you? How can I use this event to make me a stronger Christian?

We must not live in fear. Sometimes we may even try to bargain and plead with God to get our own way or somehow have our loved one back. I remember even asking God to take me and give Patty back. But, after thinking through that scenario, there is no way I would want someone I loved so dearly to have to walk through what I was going through. It was selfish and I was thinking only of myself.

Although we are desperate for some explanation of why we are in this valley, we cannot lower ourselves to bartering with God. Not only is it not wise, it is futile. Just know that God is near, and we can trust Him in both tragedy and triumph. His faithfulness is great. He knows what He's doing and He's got this.

When we lose a loved one, a spouse in particular, there is real pain; almost physical. It gives new meaning to the scripture in Genesis 2:24 where God was speaking about the marriage union that says, *"the two shall become one flesh."* When that sacred union is ripped apart, it is likened to a set of conjoined twins being separated. As the surgeon cuts them apart and the raw flesh is exposed they lose part of their identity and are no longer the same. The doctor, with all his surgical skill, stitches and sews the wounds up but the scars will always be there.

When I lost my wife, Patty, one of the first things that hit me was that my identity had changed. In an instant, I was no longer "Doug and Patty" but just "Doug." As this happens to each of us, we are immediately tossed into that sea of sorrow where the waves and water toss us back and forth like a drunken man trying to walk on a moving sidewalk.

It would be so easy to just give up at this point and lie down. We have lost a part of ourselves and feel like there is no escape. The sorrow is real and the wounds immeasurably tender. But know we are not going through this alone. Isaiah 53:3 tells us that Jesus himself was a Man of sorrows and acquainted with grief. No matter what we are feeling or how much turmoil our emotions are in, Jesus has already been there and blazed a trail for us to follow to get us to the other side of this tragedy. His arms are open toward you right now and He is calling you to Himself. He understands your pain and wants to wrap you up in His love and hold you tight. Let Him.

During this time of grieving, be reminded that God does not waste anything. As we lay our lives at His feet, He takes us, along with our pain, and uses us for His glory. He uses the gifts and talents that we expect but I believe it gives Him special delight to use the parts of us we thought invaluable. The mundane and broken parts of our lives end up being the very thing He sets His favor upon and where He gets His greatest pleasure. God is looking for people who are willing to offer Him everything; gifts, talents, abilities and even brokenness and pain. Jesus wants it all and He will cause you to see the beauty in how He uses all for His glory.

The coral just under the surface represents all our fears. Fear of the unknown, what is lurking just below the surface, will destroy you if you let it. If you are a believer, then you know that the devil is the author of all fear. He plants these reefs in our lives to bring harm and destruction any way he can. If we give in to fear, we risk being sucked into that vortex of darkness and becoming consumed by it.

When we put ourselves in the safety of God's hands and we are surrounded by His love, the Bible tells us that His perfect love casts out all fear. Hide yourself in Him today and He will snatch you from the grip of fear and bring you to safety.

Another thing we must do is hold on to the chair; even strap ourselves to it for this is representative of the throne of God. As long as we stay connected to God through prayer, worship, and relationship we will be saved. The Bible declares in Psalm 61 that God is our refuge and strong tower and that He protects those who run to Him for safety. This relationship is vitally important. It is more important than that relationship we had with the one we recently lost. And, it is kind of an odd relationship as well.

I have seen on social media, often, little video clips of two animals that should not be friendly with one another, a pig and a cat or a deer and a dog, and it always amazes me that they toss aside their natural tendencies to be at odds and enter, what appears to be, a caring relationship based on trust and faith in the other.

And, so it is with our relationship with God. We, as humans, are bent toward sin and God is completely holy. How can a God who cannot even look at sin want a relationship with us who are sinners? Because, He created us for that exact purpose. He desires to be in relationship with you and me. He loved us enough to allow His son, Jesus, to take our place in the path of His own wrath and judgement against sin. And that, my friend, is the gospel message in a nutshell.

When we accept what God has done to reconcile us to Himself, that is the good news. That is what faith looks like. Colossians 1:23 tells us if we continue in this faith, grounded and settled, we will not be moved away from the gospel. We must fix our eyes on Jesus, the author and perfecter of our faith. He is the key to our relationship with God. He is the doorway. And, if our faith is weak, the Word of God holds the answer. The Bible tells us that faith comes by hearing and hearing by the Word of God. Dig into it; find out what it says. Plant it deep into your heart. The Psalmist says in chapter 119, verses 11-13, *"I have hidden your word in my heart that I might not sin against you. Praise be to you, Lord; teach me your decrees. With my lips I recount all the laws that come from your mouth."*

Wow! Not only does the Psalmist read and study what the word of God says, he also hides it in his heart. Why? To keep him from sin. Not only does he hide it in his heart, but, his mouth recounts all that God has spoken to him on a daily basis.

I am not a "name it and claim it" kind of person but there is power in our words. The Bible tells us that life and death are in the power of the tongue. I encourage you to find verses that speak to your situation and ones you find uplifting or encouraging and begin to speak them aloud. You can start with this one. *"Surely the arm of the Lord is not too short to save, nor His ear too dull to hear,"* Isaiah 59:1. Go ahead; say it aloud right now before you go any further.

What is this island called grief? Although this island is not a physical island, it can be an intensely real and emotional place. When we wake up one day on this beach, feeling trapped by the waves of sorrow in front, the mountain of adversity behind and the heavy clouds of depression above us, it can make us feel incredibly isolated.

Even though others are there with us on the beach, we feel like we are the only ones and it can be extremely lonely. There will be times of reflection and remembrance and a lot of the time, these memories create that sense of loss and are what propel us into the loneliness and depression. Remember Philippians 4:13. *"I can do all things through Christ who gives me strength."* Look for encouragement from God above. Maybe it will be in the form of a hot meal in a floating box or a fishing trip. He is the one who will give us exactly what we need, when we need it.

When we take time to look at things through God's eyes, then we will see with clarity all that he wants us to see. We are not the only ones hurting and experiencing this loss. We must reach out to our friends and family members; they, too, have lost a husband, wife, brother, sister, cousin, daughter, son, etc.

It is a good thing to remember. It will be painful at first but just like the shards of glass on the beach, each memory will become smooth on the edges over time. And, with every passing wave more beautiful, joyful and less painful.

Seeing others grieve with us is reassuring somehow. Possibly it is in knowing that when we have finished our race here, that we, too, will not be forgotten. It also lets us know that we are not alone in the grieving process.

Patty's life impacted literally hundreds of people for positive change. She was a prayer warrior and anyone who knew her knew that if they called on her, she would stop whatever it was that she was doing and pray; sometimes on the phone, other times driving to the home of the one in distress. Her life impacted others and this encourages us to live in such a way that we have an impact on others long after we have left this world.

The clouds represent the depression that tries to cover us during this time and tries to block out the sun from shining on our lives. We cannot not let depression overtake us. The best weapon for this is the word of God. It will not return to God empty but will accomplish what He sent it to do. And, that is to set us free from depression and fear and every other bondage.

The Bible tells us in Nehemiah 8:10 that the joy of the Lord is our strength. Joy is not necessarily happiness. Happiness is a fleeting, temporary condition that has to do with our emotions and the comfort of our fleshly body. Happiness is a wimp. It will run and hide at the first sign of trouble. Joy, on the other hand, is tough. It is a vital spiritual force that is not based on our outward circumstances, but upon the true condition of our hearts.

Isaiah 61 tells us that the Lord Himself will give us joy for mourning. He gives us His joy and takes the mourning to Himself. Some of us are in the middle of a trial of grief right now and may think it will never end. Psalm 30:5 says, *"Weeping may endure for a night, but joy comes in the morning."* Just know that the night won't last; daybreak is just after the darkest part of the night and when we are planted and rooted in a firm relationship with God, joy comes. And, it is an unshakeable, unspeakable joy, full of glory.

The cave in my story is a cave of despair. We crawl in there and feel protected and hidden from the pain of the world somehow. We have no desire to see or do anything. It's okay to crawl in there. It's okay to visit this place. I believe this is God's way of protecting us while we are most vulnerable. The tears shed here allow for crystal-clear vision to enable us to see family and friends through wiser, stronger eyes. The darkness of the cave allows even the smallest slivers of light to be magnified and directs us to the source of all hope. It is important to note that if we are hiding in a cave out of fear or despair, God is not afraid to come into that place and visit with us for a while. His ultimate goal, though, is to walk us through to the mountaintop and get us back into the calling He has placed on our lives. The cave is okay to visit but let's not set up camp there.

Of course, Grandpa, is a likeness of our Heavenly Father. He is kind, gentle, forgiving, and loving. He brings us alongside and teaches us and encourages us. Through the grief, He is giving us a new purpose and a fresh calling. When we look at our situation through his eyes, and put his glasses on, we begin to see with clarity His plan and purpose for what it is we are going through. His plan is perfect, and we can have absolute trust in Him; as absolute as a mother's words when she speaks them with her hands on her hips.

Now, the mountain of adversity is the only thing standing between you and your victory over the enemy's relentless attacks on your resolve to get through this trial. There is adversity and it is not always easy, but, God is beckoning to us right now to start the climb up this mountain; to begin the upward turn. Our lives, even though different than before, are waiting on us just above the clouds. So, let's climb. We can do it together. We are surrounded by a great cloud of witnesses who are joining with God in his encouragements to us.

Your loved one is now included in the throngs of people peering over the edge of heaven and with millions of united voices they are yelling their encouragements to me and you. *"Come on! You can make it! It is worth the struggle. Oh, the joy we have experienced. No more bondage, no more pain, no more tears, no more sickness; we are free, and it is too great to describe!"* Just imagine for a moment your loved one standing there in the great cloud of witnesses, shouting words of encouragement to you, and, Jesus walking up and putting his arm around their shoulders and joining in the cheering. He is smiling broadly because He loves us much more than we know. He really does love us and wants more than anything else in all creation to have us with Him.

Once we get above the clouds and back into the remnants of our lives there will be a time of adjustment and a reconstruction of sorts. What does our new life look like. We can relate it to a house that has just been through a terrible storm. There was much damage to the structure and the home must be partially rebuilt or completely demolished and start from scratch. So it is with our lives. We have to discover how our new life will look. We must build and strengthen the structure, paint and decorate it and make it a home again.

We can't lose hope. Hope is a good thing. Maybe one of the best of things. That is the substance of our faith. For when we have hope, no good thing ever dies. And even though our loved one is no longer with us here on this earth, they will never die because we keep their memory with us. Every time we share a memory with others, we deposit a fragment of our memories with them and they, too will remember. We also have the promise that we will once again be together. This hope is as an anchor for the soul, firm and secure. This is the hope that is only found in a relationship with Jesus.

I like this quote from the movie, *"Shawshank Redemption."* It is a statement from the character Andy Dufresne who was wrongly accused of murdering his wife and was sentenced to life in prison.

He didn't deserve to be there, didn't do anything wrong to end up there and certainly didn't want to be there. He was under the oppressive tyrannical rule of a criminal warden. As he planned his escape, he stated to Red, his friend and fellow inmate, *"It all comes down to a simple choice, really... Get busy livin' or get busy dyin'."*

Some of us are in this same circumstance. We are in a situation that we had no control over, that we did not deserve, and we did not invite into our lives. Yet, the enemy of our soul wants to keep us imprisoned on this island of grief and sorrow and cover us with depression just like the warden did to Andy.

But, we have a choice. You have a choice. It is not up to anyone else. Today is your day to choose. Jesus said in John 10:10, *"I have come that they may have life, and life more abundantly."* Will you choose to live? Will you climb the mountain? I pray that you choose life. We are all cheering for you!

ABOUT THE AUTHOR

Doug Johnson is a Christian father and grandfather who, like so many others, lost his spouse too early in life to breast cancer. Although this is his first book, the concept and storyline came to him in the days and weeks after his wife passed away. He began to write as an outlet to pass the time and help him deal with the grief he was experiencing himself. His prayer is that this little book will help you if you are battling the emotions tied to the loss of someone special and cause you to discover the call and plan that God has for your life as well.

www.ingramcontent.com/pod-product-compliance
Lightning Source LLC
Chambersburg PA
CBHW070636030426
42337CB00020B/4038